# Give a
# Cat
# a Home

Also available

Give a Dog a Home

# Give a Cat a Home

National Trust

*For Mum and Gavin, who always help*
*above and beyond the call of duty.*
*Thank you, love Span x*

987654321
First published in 2008
Reprinted in 2010
Packaged by Susanna Geoghegan for
National Trust Books
10, Southcombe Street
London W14 0RA

An imprint of Anova Books Company Ltd

ISBN 978-1-906388-20-1

Little Dog Laughed Ltd
22a Parker Centre, Mansfield Road
Derby, DE21 4SZ
Tel: 01332 290605 Fax: 01332 290778
www.thelittledoglaughed.co.uk

Printed in China by Hung Hing

# Introduction

## Battersea Dogs & Cats Home was founded in 1860 by a courageous lady called Mary Tealby.

Being concerned by the large numbers of street dogs in London, she opened the Home in a stable yard in Holloway. In 1871 we moved to our present site in Battersea and started caring for cats in 1883. We now have three sites: at Battersea in south-west London, Old Windsor in Berkshire and Brands Hatch, Kent.

Since 1860 the Home has cared for over three million lost or abandoned dogs and cats. We aim never to turn away a dog or cat in need of our help and each year we take in over 12,000 of them. Many of the lost animals are reunited with their owners within just a few days. Others require more intensive help by our veterinary clinic or behaviour staff to help with their individual problems and this means that their stay with us can be a lot longer.

Battersea's staff and volunteers are some of the most dedicated people you will ever meet. They go to extraordinary lengths to help the animals, whether it is finding the perfect new family or working home, fostering a dog or cat or hand-rearing tiny kittens every four hours throughout the night. They deal with the best and worst of situations with care, compassion and feeling.

None of our work would be possible without the kindness and generosity of our supporters. Battersea Dogs & Cats Home is a registered charity and we rely totally on donations to fund our work. This is one of the reasons that we were so delighted to have the opportunity to collaborate with The Little Dog Laughed. The funds raised from each book will directly help the dogs and cats in our care and those yet to come to us.

It is wonderful to see in print the stories of our wonderful ex-residents, and especially to see how they have changed and touched the lives of their new owners.

On behalf of all the two and four-legged residents at the Home we would like to thank everyone at The Little Dog Laughed for choosing Battersea Dogs & Cats Home and especially Anna Danielle; her illustrations bring the dogs and cats to life. Thank you to the staff and owners who contributed their stories and their dogs and cats who sat patiently for their paw-traits!

And, of course, thank you for purchasing this book and for supporting Battersea Dogs & Cats Home.

# Phoebe

## It's hard to believe that the Phoebe we see today is the very same cat that came home from Battersea with the Hinkley family nearly five years ago.

No longer timid, nervous or withdrawn, Phoebe is possibly the most affectionate, friendly cat you will ever meet.

If you had the time, she would gladly let you fuss her all day. She places her head under the lips of anyone willing to give her a kiss and will leave it there indefinitely, soaking up as many kisses as the giver can manage before they run out of breath.

She is a true lady, incredibly pretty and sleek with a beautiful coat and gorgeous colourings. Her nickname is 'Princess' – and for good reason.

Every morning without fail she sits on the dressing table and watches Hilary apply her make-up. She even has her breakfast up there. When Hilary has finished she then has to pretend to put some make-up on Phoebe's face and she dabs her cheeks with a brush which she keeps especially for her, telling her all the while how beautiful she is. Phoebe will not leave Hilary's side until they have been through this ritual.

This affection did not occur overnight, and with every milestone conquered another took its place. It took two years to be able to approach Phoebe in the garden. Whilst she was fine indoors, if they spoke to her outside she would run. Nowadays it's impossible to hang out the washing or do a spot of gardening without Phoebe appearing from nowhere and demanding more love.

# Millie

## Millie joined the Hinkley family a year after Phoebe.

She was badly neglected by her owner and the Hinkleys quickly offered her a loving home. Another tortoiseshell tabby, she is just as beautiful as Phoebe, but there the similarity ends.

Millie is a complete tomboy and a house-wrecker, but she has bags of character and charm and is always forgiven. Millie is also exceptionally intelligent and usually one step ahead of the Hinkleys, especially when it comes to flea application.

Even when Hilary entered the room with the pipette hidden up her sleeve, Millie was off like a shot. So, in the kitchen, out of Millie's sight, they tried pouring the liquid onto a teaspoon and whilst someone fussed over Millie, surreptitiously brushing her fur forward, Hilary would race in and tip the liquid straight on. However, this tactic's success was short lived. Whether she smelt a rat when her fur was stroked the wrong way or could actually smell the lotion as Hilary got nearer is unknown.

Either way the whole process is a complete nightmare and Millie makes no apologies for putting up a struggle. Phoebe, on the other hand, is far too ladylike to make a fuss and whilst she is aware that something unpleasant has occurred, the most she gives is a disapproving look.

Millie and Phoebe are great company for each other despite their chalk and cheese personalities and the Hinkleys simply couldn't imagine one without the other.

# Freddie

## Freddie is a quirky Battersea special.

She is a ginger and white female and quite rare as generally cats with that colouring are male.

Lucinda dearly wanted a cat but waited until she had her own home before adopting. She made her boyfriend dress smartly for the rehoming interview and told him to 'keep quiet' as she was the experienced cat owner and he might blow their chances. They passed with flying colours and Lucinda was thrilled to glimpse the note 'really good home with lots of experience' on their form.

It was on their third visit to Battersea that Lucinda saw Freddie. She was in pen number twenty-two, in a covered cat basket. Lucinda had mentally decided against a ginger and white cat as her previous cat

had been of that colouring. She didn't want to try and replace the irreplaceable, but Freddie had already stolen her heart.

On her first night at home, Freddie polished off a plate of chicken tikka masala and has begged and pestered for titbits ever since. Sitting on the arm of the sofa, she'll crane her neck to see what's on offer and meow in little chirps until one of them gives in. Nine times out of ten it's Lucinda who cracks first.

Freddie keeps her affections for those she knows and wisely avoids wasting time on strangers. Everything she does is on her terms but her love for Lucinda is unquestionable and as long as the food keeps coming Freddie is a very happy cat.

# Lola

## There's a misconception that one goes to Battersea to choose a pet.

Nothing could be further from the truth. Take Lola: she knew at first glance that Laura and Mark Oliver would be the lucky ones and put on a heart-winning performance from her kitty cabin. Then she firmly turned her back on the rest of the potential servants and waited for her carriage to be called.

Life really does revolve around Lola. Mark and Laura work long hours to keep a roof over her head and expensive food in her bowl. The wrong food receives a frosty look of disgust and the silent treatment until the crime has been rectified.

Lola seems like your average black and white cat. However, unlike most cats Lola adores water and often sits out in the rain. She also loves heights and demanded a penthouse pad above the kitchen wall units. Maybe this is not so unusual in itself until you witness her death-defying, vertical, head-first decent. Add in the excessively fluffy tail and you'd be forgiven for thinking 'squirrel' but she is in fact a Norwegian Forest Cat.

Lola dislikes being picked up and despises lap cats. However, if you've been good she will allow you to stroke her. Lola fully appreciates that good staff are hard to find and readily admits that she made an excellent choice in the Olivers. Thankfully, they feel the same and are happily committed to a life of long, dedicated service.

# Fish

## Star of YouTube and extremely popular on Facebook, Fish is a high-climbing, attention-seeking Red Point, who has all the yowl of a Siamese and none of the grace.

A true clown and gorgeously ugly, he is named after Emma's ex-boyfriend who bears an uncanny resemblance to the young cat.

Emma's original cat Kevin, a jet black Oriental, failed to return home one night and after six long weeks Emma could bear an empty flat no longer. She viewed the Battersea website, successfully adopted Fish and then welcomed Kevin home, unharmed, a week later!

A film producer for a London advertising agency, Emma is a celluloid addict. With a camera permanently by her side, if it moves she films it and if it doesn't, she still films it. Fish does whatever he can to ensure the focus is always on him:

he is the biggest scene-stealer and disrupter imaginable and will stoop to any level to gain success. Climbing over cameras and lights, Fish managed to ruin ten hours of filming by getting his head stuck under a sofa and howling for attention.

A thief of baby clothes and packed lunches, Fish also enjoys parading up and down his Victorian terrace rooftop pretending he's stuck. He has a weakness for 'smoothies' (but only the banana and coconut flavour) and constantly raids the fridge.

Fish adds untold amounts of stress to Emma's life but she secretly adores him: he is her completely loveable pain in the bum.

# The Lloyd Family

## Jean Lloyd is a very special lady. An infant school teacher, she nursed her husband for ten years when he suffered a brain stem stroke.

Her relationship with Battersea's Old Windsor site developed as a result of caring for Julian and the combined age of all Jean's Battersea rescues adds up to a staggering one hundred and ten years.

Poppy was the first cat to join the Lloyd household. She came from work colleagues and was intended as a bed cat for Julian. A beautiful silver tortoiseshell tabby, she excelled at her job, curling into his arms and often sleeping between his legs.

Now twelve, Poppy is the head feline of the house and keeps the Battersea misfits in order. Binnie joined them next – named after his addiction for sorting through bins and bags. He had belonged

to an old lady who had gone into care. A Felix lookalike, Binnie is a real character.

The first rescue to come from Battersea was actually a dog. With all the lifting involved in Julian's care, Jean's daughter Rebecca had trapped a muscle, a condition very common amongst the nursing profession. Effective treatment included dog walking, so the Lloyds made their way to Old Windsor and returned home with Emily, a collie cross. Totally spoilt, Emily had been a companion for someone suffering with a mental illness, but no longer able to cope, they had given her to the Home. Emily did the trick and when Rebecca got married, Emily moved with her.

# Sophie

## Jean adopts the ancient, broken and damaged cats that are unlikely to find good homes.

Battersea have Jean's telephone number on redial: she is a ray of hope when all hope seems lost.

Knowing these cats' time might be short and sadness is inevitable, Jean draws comfort from the knowledge that she can give them security, love and a little bit of happiness in whatever time they have left.

Sadly, ten years after his stroke, Jean's husband Julian passed away. Jean was left with lots of towelling that had been used in his care. Knowing that the Home always needed blankets and towels she took them up to Old Windsor.

Sophie, originally named Sylvie, a sixteen-ish black and white cat had previously been owned by a divorced gentleman. He gave her in to the Home when his job meant Sophie was alone for long periods of time. Her card had read 'Wanted, lap and garden, take me home today' so Jean did just that.

Sophie reached the fine old age of eighteen and enjoyed two happy, loving years before passing away having suffered with a thyroid problem.

# Spice

## Next came Sugar and Spice, seventeen and eighteen respectively.

Tortoiseshells, they were found together in a bin shed. It's unknown how long they'd been shut in there. Sugar had a renal problem and tragically died just seven weeks after being adopted. Originally semi-feral, Jean slowly won Spice's trust and can now pick her up and cuddle her. However, she still refuses to let the grooming brush anywhere near her. It was such a wonderful moment when Spice finally purred with pleasure and it is a delight to see her enjoying the garden. Sniffing the flowers and listening to the bird songs, Spice spends hours outside.

Spice is now blind and Jean believes she may also be suffering from senile dementia as she has taken to sitting on the stairs and howling very loudly.

As long as Spice continues to enjoy the garden, eat her food and is in no discomfort then the Lloyd household is happy to bear the vocal outbursts.

Tabatha arrived next, an indoor cat who weighed a massive eight kilos. Resembling a footstool rather than a cat, her fur was matted and her teeth were falling out. A pretty-looking tabby, Tabatha is actually a Devon Rex and had lived with an elderly lady who went into care. On a strict diet, Tabatha has often been caught sneaking into the kitchen hunting for snacks but to date she has lost over three kilos and is a happier cat as a result. Now able to run and clean herself, the difference in her personality is amazing.

# Melody

## Next to take shelter in the Lloyd household was Brandy.

Given to Old Windsor with her sister Shandy, their information stated that both cats kept messing in the house. Tragically, Shandy was put to sleep suffering from a major heart defect and Battersea called Jean to tell her of Brandy's plight. So Jean fetched Brandy and brought her home and to Brandy's credit, she has never once messed in the house. A feisty tortoiseshell with a mind of her own, she has a marvellously loud deep purr and loves to settle down on Jean's bed for the night.

In her spare time Jean crochets blankets which are most welcome at the cattery. It was when she dropped some off at Old Windsor that she came back with Melody. The staff told Jean to pop her head round the door of the chill-out room 'just to have a look'. The room was completely pink. Pink cushions, pink blankets, pink toys and there in the middle of all this girliness was Melody, a black and white stray wearing a massive pink bow. Approximately thirteen years old, Melody was quite a nervous cat and would lash out for no real reason if she felt in the slightest bit threatened. This put people off adopting her but Jean came to the rescue.

Independent Melody is beginning to calm down and get used to a loving environment but is far too long in the tooth to completely dispose of her feisty moments.

# Dexter & Telissa

## More blankets later and home came Dexter and Telissa.

Approximately seventeen years old, the litter mates had been given in to the home with a number of other cats. Dexter, black with white socks, has cauliflower ears and a third-degree heart murmur and Telissa, a pretty tabby, is profoundly deaf. They have the sweetest natures, always eating from the same bowl and are the gentlest cats Jean has ever known.

Sharing her home with eight cats, the last thing you'd expect Jean to do is adopt a dog. However, on her doctor's advice – to help with her osteoporosis – she went to Old Windsor looking for a small slow dog that liked cats. She returned with a large Labrador cross with a mild hip problem. Red, renamed Freddie, was given in to the Home with his brother

Blue. Their owner had passed away and rather tragically Blue then died whilst in kennels, leaving Freddie all alone.

Freddie keeps a healthy distance between himself and the gang. The cats reacted with indifference to the presence of a lower species in their home. With eight cats and one dog you may wonder what the neighbours think but thankfully all is harmonious. Jean's neighbour is a veterinary nurse and with a menagerie of animals herself they could quite easily open an animal care centre between them.

Battersea are very grateful for Jean's dedication to the broken, old and lonely. Without her, it is unlikely that these cats would now be enjoying such a happy, loving home.

# Molly

## Molly is a moody, vocal, tantrum-throwing little white cat who thinks she's human and constantly gets into scrapes.

Claire and Pete Palmer wouldn't want her any other way.

When they went to choose a cat from Battersea Old Windsor they hadn't fallen instantly in love and resigned themselves to returning on another day.

Then out of the corner of her eye, Claire saw a tiny white kitten, climbing the bars of her cage like a monkey and meowing with such enthusiasm that it was impossible to walk away. However, Molly had already found a home, but they put their names down in reserve, just in case. And 'just in case' paid off.

Originally Molly had lived with a family whose small child kept pulling her tail, and as a consequence she hated having

her back touched. It took a long time to gain Molly's trust and even now she sometimes throws a tantrum and reverts back to her old ways.

Molly is always getting into mischief. She's suffered bee stings from bumble bee hunting, fallen in ponds, got stuck on the roof and covered herself head to foot in black soot after hiding in a charcoal bag.

She loves tasty food and appears from nowhere when she smells bacon and eggs being cooked and goes positively giddy if Spaghetti Bolognese is on the menu. When she is in the mood, Molly is a great lap cat and very affectionate. Claire and Pete adore her quirkiness and never quite know what she'll do next.

29

# Stevie

## Jeanette Reynolds sadly said goodbye to Sam, her beloved cat who was blind and brain damaged.

Self confessed 'cat mad', she was already sharing her home with three rescue cats: Marvin the domesticated feral, George the sickly tabby and voiceless Wesley, who was saved from strangulation as a kitten but left with no meows.

Wanting to utilise her experience of caring for disabled cats, Jeanette registered with Battersea and two months later received a phone call informing her that not one but two cats needed a loving home.

Gypsy had one eye with little sight and his brother Tinka had no eyes at all. The boys had been gifted to the Home with no real explanation. Their mother had cat flu when she was pregnant and both kittens were born with the illness as a result. This damaged their sight: sadly, a common symptom of the disease. Jeanette went to meet the boys and immediately fell in love. She was now the only female in a five-male household.

Tinka was renamed Stevie. He is such a sweet little chap who loves to play with his toys. If he ever loses one his brother takes it to him. Wandering around the garden and soaking up the sunshine on a hot day is his favourite pastime. Stevie is best friends with George the tabby and they are always together, practically joined at the hip.

Jeanette feels very privileged to be able to care for Stevie and Gabe (Gypsy) and couldn't imagine her home without them.

# Gabe

## Jeanette renamed Gypsy, Gabe as he really is her guardian angel.

He only has one eye and the vision in that is very poor. However, Gabe does venture outside and is quite the local celebrity with the neighbours. They keep watch over him as he explores the cul-de-sac and if he ever loses his way or gets confused Marvin, the domesticated feral, locates him and escorts him safely home.

Gabe is incredibly affectionate and Jeanette doesn't go anywhere without him. If she walks to the shops, Gabe goes with her. If Jeanette pops round to her friends for a cup of tea, Gabe follows her down the road and then sits in the rain or shine waiting for Jeanette to come out. Gabe then walks her home. Living with blind or disabled

cats takes very little extra effort. The only difference in Jeanette's care for Gabe and Stevie is to keep their bowls and litter tray in the same place. It upsets and confuses them if they're moved. When Jeanette picks them up for a cuddle she has to put them down in exactly the same spot to avoid them becoming disorientated.

The boys' blindness actually encourages Jeanette to keep on top of her housework: she is careful to put away the vacuum cleaner and never leaves mugs or shoes lying around for the boys to run into.

Stevie and Gabe are wonderful cats and shining examples that cats with special needs should never be overlooked.

# Pedro

## Pedro was having a run of very bad luck.

Given to Battersea when his owners emigrated, he was also carrying a leg wound after being shot with an air rifle. Battersea's veterinary team investigated and found the pellet still embedded in his leg. Then he caught cat flu and became seriously ill, spending a long time in quarantine.

Thankfully, Pedro's luck was about to change: Alex Johnson and Lisa Burr wanted a cat. They had just bought their first house with a garden and the only thing missing was a rescue moggie. After viewing Battersea's website Lisa declared Pedro was the one. Despite living closer to the Old Windsor site they trekked across London to see Pedro.

The journey wasn't wasted. Jet black with little white gloves on his feet, a white chest and a soft pink belly, Pedro was definitely the one.

However, his profile sounded high maintenance: no young children and no other animals, probably difficult to settle. Thankfully he was the complete opposite. The minute he stepped out of his cat carrier it was obvious he was home. Purring and rubbing up against their legs, Pedro was a dream cat. Having both grown up surrounded by cats most of their lives, Alex and Lisa had never known a cat like him.

Pedro loves people and is very affectionate. He is incredibly confident and vocal. All positive attributes – except that is, when he sits outside Alex and Lisa's bedroom and starts his version of a dawn chorus at some ungodly hour of the morning!

# Bijou

**Apollo, Roxy and Bijou arrived at Battersea's Old Windsor cattery when their owner died.**

Apollo, a big ginger tom, Roxy, a large black and white girl and Bijou a petite tabby with three legs, were placed in one of the chill-out rooms. Designed to create a homely environment with armchairs, blankets and music, the rooms are a tremendous help with cats that are part of a family group or unable to cope in smaller pens. Although Roxy had a mild heart murmur, they passed their medical and were ready for adoption.

Unfortunately, not many visitors want three senior cats, one with a heart murmur and one with only three legs. The weeks turned into months and the hapless trio became a permanent fixture at Battersea.

Finally, the decision was made to split the group. It was apparent that Apollo and Roxy couldn't be parted but Bijou was the more independent of the three. Kennelhand Amy Stallwood had bonded with Bijou and quickly offered her a home. The decision worked: two weeks later, Apollo and Roxy were adopted.

Bijou settled in well, taking her new life, and even the stairs, all in her somewhat wobbly stride. She never lets anything hold her back and is always climbing into boxes, a suitcase or open drawer. Sometimes, if startled, Bijou will run off as fast as she can at a sideways angle, earning her the affectionate nickname of Hobbledy-Pop. After a delayed start, Bijou has definitely fallen on all three feet!

# Beaker

Robin became a cat socialiser for Battersea whilst recovering from a serious car accident.

Suffering anxiety attacks amongst crowds and on public transport, Robin was practically housebound. His family rescued a kitten and Kato's arrival marked the turning point in Robin's recovery. Caring for Kato rebuilt Robin's confidence and his spirits soared. Then, a house move put him in walking distance of the Home and so Robin volunteered his time, hoping to put his experience to some use.

Beaker, a two-week-old kitten, was being attacked by his litter mates. He was removed for his own safety and Robin became his new mum. Beaker needed hand weaning and a toothbrush was used to imitate a mother's cleaning tongue.

Beaker was unable to generate his own body heat so Robin

placed him in a special sleeping bag which he hung from his shoulder, thus keeping Beaker warm with his own body. Beaker happily shared his hot water bottle at bedtime with his new soft toy litter mates and was soon bounding around the house, practising his pouncing, learning to wash himself and use his litter tray.

However, some lessons only a mother can teach and Beaker has developed a few quirky traits. He prefers sitting on shoulders to laps, choosing to interact with the world at human eye level.

Four years on Robin realised that all the while he had been rehabilitating the cats, his own fears of the wider world had also evaporated under a blanket of soothing purrs.

# Tabitha

## Little was known about Tabitha when she arrived at Battersea other than the fact that her owner had died.

At nearly eighteen, she had missing teeth, no hair around her neck, a weeping eye, hyperthyroidism, kidney problems and cat flu. There had been little interest in rehoming her and she had been at the Home for over six months.

Michelle Bartsch, Battersea's Events Officer and a real softie when it comes to sad stories, fell in love with Tabitha's decrepit feebleness and offered her a home. Her constant cat flu, which may never clear up, means she sneezes large amounts of mucus everywhere. A test of love, especially when one is just falling asleep!

Tabitha can't groom herself properly and smells as a result, so once a month she enjoys a lovely warm pampering bath.

Her favourite resting spot is on the newly washed laundry which hardly ever gets folded for fear of Tabitha's wrath should they accidentally wake her. She also drools rather a lot and meows non-stop for attention or food.

However, Tabitha is very affectionate and will follow Michelle's husband, Chris, everywhere until he sits down, then she commandeers his lap for the night. She has a rather precarious habit of crawling under the cushions and throws on the sofa and as a consequence has endured a few squashings along the way.

Despite being cranky, snotty, smelly and a total pain, Tabitha is very much part of the Bartsch family and they adore her completely.

# Thames

### Thames, a stray kitten, was found by the river and taken to Battersea's Old Windsor site.

He soon became a staff favourite and earned himself the privileged position of resident moggie. He spent his days relaxing under his special tree, cheekily outstretched in full view of the others in the cattery.

Lorna was a kennelhand and like everybody else completely adored Thames. He had such big beautiful eyes and wonderfully large paws. She often wished she could take him home. As the years passed, staff decided Thames needed a retirement home and Lorna's wish came true. He settled into his new home, finding a new spot under a fern by the pond. From there he could survey his kingdom and keep a close eye on the fish. Thames is

also known as Boss. He is so laid back, he doesn't bat an eyelid when the local 'wise guys' try to encroach on his territory. One stern look and they're gone, the Don always calm and collected.

Age and arthritis mean he can't chase birds but he pretends he can't be bothered. He loves sleeping in puzzle box lids and since he went deaf, snores very loudly. Recently, Thames was on the move again, to a home by the sea. He was completely unfazed by the move: so long as Lorna had his chicken freshly prepared, all was right in his world. Adored by all, Thames is a shining testament to the joy and love an older cat can bring.

# Tibby

## Miss Brass was fourteen when she adopted her first pet from Battersea in 1929.

Gyp the mongrel was her birthday present. Five shillings of furry intelligence, she took him home on the top deck of the number twelve tram.

Miss Brass remembers a very different BDCH in the 1930s: a mass of dogs running freely in two large yards, dogs in one, bitches in the other. She chose her dog and waited the statutory seven days, hoping and praying no one came to claim him. That was the beginning of a lifetime's commitment to Battersea rescues.

Miss Brass's latest housemate is a cat called Tibby. A dark ginger, female tortoiseshell, Tibby is a hunter and regularly brings Miss Brass a variety of wildlife to admire and experience at close range. When Tibby hurtles into

the house at full speed, Miss Brass knows there will be something to deal with – usually a petrified frog tucked behind the sofa.

Once, a squirrel shot past her into the lounge closely followed by Tibby in hot pursuit. The squirrel sat for the entire evening on the curtain pole. Eventually, after twenty-four hours of little success, she called the RSPCA to come to its rescue, much to Tibby's disappointment.

Miss Brass locks all her inner doors as Tibby can open them and frequently leaves no china ornament unturned in her quest to catch buzzing flies. Tibby's living gifts for Miss Brass are an affectionate 'thank you' for providing her with a loving, safe home.

# Amber

**Renowned portrait artist Clare Shenstone was very surprised to receive a phone call from Battersea Dogs & Cats Home saying they had found a cat for her.**

Completely unaware that she had even been looking for one, Clare later discovered that her young daughter, Georgie, had written a heart-tugging letter to Battersea requesting they find her a cat. Her mum had two, Scally and Wag, but Georgie wanted one of her own and it didn't matter if it was old, deaf, blind or only had three legs, just so long as it was hers to love and cherish.

So off they went to Battersea. This was going to be a disaster! Clare was just wondering how on earth she was going to leave without bringing them all home when Georgie announced she had found her cat. Clare tried

to explain that a cat had already been chosen for her but Georgie insisted this was the one.

Sadly her chosen cat had been reserved. When they announced their arrival to the cattery staff and asked to see the cat, they were taken straight back to Georgie's cat. It had been reserved for her!

Amber is a pedigree British Red. Amazingly pretty with fluffy, mid-length fur, she was found abandoned in a box in a kitchen. She instantly bonded with Scally and Wag, readily adopting all their Siamese traits. Georgie was delighted – at last she had her very own cat.

# Mary

## Four years later Georgie told her mum about William and Mary, two Siamese cats on the Battersea website.

A half brother and sister, their owner had been taken into care. Both cats had lived a very sheltered existence and were not coping in the cattery environment. They desperately needed new homes. Having adopted rescue Siamese all her life, Clare phoned Battersea immediately and arranged to collect them the following day.

On her arrival she discovered William had suffered a heart attack overnight and Mary, who was with him when he died, was in trauma and had been placed on a drip. Three days later, knowing that Siamese respond better amongst their own, Clare collected Mary and took her home to meet the others.

Mary, a chocolate point, was painfully thin and terrified. When Scally walked in, she began hissing in fear. He completely ignored her, jumped onto the bed and curled up next to her, quickly falling asleep.

That was the beginning of their love affair. Mary began to recover and they soon fell head over heels in love and have been devoted to each other ever since. Mary has a funny little habit of licking Scally's tail, holding it gently between her paws and grooming it all morning. By lunchtime it is completely soaked but Scally doesn't seem to mind.

All the Shenstone cats have a glorious life and often wander in and out of the studio, casting a critical eye over Clare's latest work and throwing in the odd clattered distraction to add to the creative mix.

# TC

## When 10kg TC, aka Top Cat, arrived at Battersea, she was a thoroughly miserable sight.

Given in to the Home because of her lack of fun, it was decided TC should join Poppy and Tiger as official Battersea office cats.

It was Sarah Bradbury's job to help TC shed the pounds. She was put on a special diet and had to walk around the offices before mealtime. Everyone knew to keep away from TC at feeding time. She would wind herself up before she was fed and swing around the ankles of any unsuspecting member of staff who dared to walk past her!

TC always commandeered the best bed, even if it was already occupied, gently nudging out the intruder until she was comfortable. TC is also incredibly laid back: on one occasion the

office had a mouse problem and on a particular lunchtime, ten mice made a break for freedom at the same moment. Poppy and Craig (another temporary office cat) sat by the hole trying to catch the mice as they came out, but TC just looked bemused as the mice scutled past her.

When TC retired she had lost over 4kg. Now on a renal diet, she occasionally gets to enjoy a chicken or prawn treat. A very solitary feline, she completely ignores Molly the dog and Colin the cat but dribbles with delight when Sarah or her husband, Clive, make a fuss of her. TC adores lying in the conservatory soaking up the sun and is a very contented old girl.

# Colin

## Colin had been living at the bottom of a garden in Kensington for two weeks when he was brought into Battersea.

Diagnosed with a grade five heart murmur and umbilical hernia, Colin was overweight with a saggy belly. He was unlikely to be rehomed due to his health problems and there was no vacancy for another office cat. Sarah had heard of his plight but felt there was little she could do.

The following weekend Sarah was showing some friends around the Home and as they entered the cattery, they saw a daft old black and white cat rolling around on his shelf enjoying the sunshine. In his excitement at seeing visitors he mistimed his roll and fell off the shelf. Sarah was smitten and Colin had a new home.

He made himself very comfortable in the conservatory and informed Sarah immediately of his dietary requirements: meat only, beef cat food whenever possible and on no account whatsoever serve him fish. Colin hates fish.

However, Colin does love people, demanding fuss in the morning and then all evening. It is quite impossible to ignore him because his purr is so loud. He is also incredibly nosey and rushes to greet anyone who enters the house, sniffing and purring as he winds himself around their legs. Despite being given only six months to live, four years later Colin is still enjoying life despite the odd senior moment and he often congratulates himself on the timing of his mistimed roll!

# Ripley

## Having lost her beloved Siamese, Merlin, to a fungal disease, Vanessa was devastated.

He had been her best friend for over twelve years and she missed him desperately.

A long time later, Vanessa's boyfriend, Alex, felt it would help to have another cat in their lives, not to replace Merlin but to make their house feel like a home again.

Browsing through the Battersea website the first cat they saw was Ripley, a Burmese cross. Vanessa adores oriental breeds and it was love at first sight. Of course, upon looking further they fell for all the other cats as well, but Ripley's appeal held fast.

A mad dash to Battersea and he was even more gorgeous than his picture; he had the silkiest fur imaginable. The adoption was put in process but then Ripley had a major setback. He'd come to Battersea with a history of leg pain. As he responded to painkillers the vet diagnosed that Ripley's leg was causing him tremendous pain and the kindest course of action would be to amputate.

Ripley's demeanour changed overnight. Pain free, he became happy, affectionate and ready for his new home. He settled well, his disability a minor issue. He loves to claw the furniture, occasionally wobbling as he does and tends to pull himself up on things with a little helpful hop rather than a jump. As he snuggles down with a paw either side of Vanessa's neck he has the contented look of the cat that definitely got the cream.

# Twiglet

## The only pet Diane Johnson's family owned when they visited Battersea Old Windsor was a rabbit.

Little did Diane know she would end up working as a receptionist for Battersea and her house would soon become a home to six cats, a St Bernard, a Newfoundland and a rough collie. Not bad for a lady who suffers with asthma and had an allergy to animal hair!

Having talked at length with the Battersea staff regarding adopting a family cat and the possible allergy reaction, Diane and her daughter Samantha were introduced to Kitty, a domestic short-haired tortoiseshell and white. After a second visit proved Diane's skin allergies were non-reactive, Kitty was renamed Twiglet and she went home with the Johnsons. Although she had been given to the Home due to

messing in the house, it transpires Twiglet hadn't had an indoor litter tray. Nine years on she is still particular about her toilet habits and will only use her litter tray if it is placed 'just so' by the side of her bed.

Twiglet is a sweet, affectionate recluse who loves the dogs but sadly gets bullied by other cats, and at times even seems scared of her own shadow.

After their first visit, Diane joined her daughter, Samantha, in volunteering their time as cat socialisers, then later took on the role of foster carer for numerous cats that needed extra care. Diane definitely got a little more than she bargained for on that innocent visit back in 1999.

# Pepsi

## Twiglet was soon followed by Pepsi and Whisky.

Pepsi, a black and white domestic short hair originally came into Battersea Old Windsor with her litter mates at just five weeks old. Found in a shed and semi-feral, they had barely received any human contact. Once in the cattery they would hide and if anyone got too close they would run up the wire surround clinging on and hissing for dear life.

Diane was a cat socialiser when Pepsi arrived and after five weeks of constant attention, Pepsi finally allowed Diane to pick her up and stroke her. Soon she was ready for rehoming and Diane quickly offered to take her. She was at home during the day and knew she could easily provide the right environment and security that Pepsi needed. Due to Pepsi's nervous nature it was felt she would benefit by being rehomed with a more confident kitten from another litter. Diane and Samantha had also spent a great deal of time with Whisky who was roughly the same age and the two cats bonded instantly.

Pepsi has grown into a loving affectionate cat but only on her terms. She is very independent, coming and going as she pleases. She chooses when she wants her food, when she wants attention and when she wants solitude. The Johnsons willingly grant Pepsi her space knowing that any affection they receive is all the more special as it is all from her own choosing.

# Whisky

## Whisky is a ginger and white domestic short hair and the complete opposite to Pepsi.

A real home cat, he adores attention, cuddles and sleeping on the bed.

Whenever Diane has fostered kittens that need extra love and care, Whisky becomes a surrogate 'mother' to them. Amazing to witness, Whisky will take over all the kittens' care needs, grooming, sleeping and playing with them.

Once, Diane took in five kittens whose mum had tragically died after swallowing a chicken bone. They were only four weeks old and still nursing. Whisky took over and kept them in line. He hardly left the house whilst they were in his care. The Johnsons had them for over five weeks and when they were ready to be rehomed Whisky took it all in his

stride – no pining for his brood, just satisfaction at a job well done. A truly remarkable cat.

Pickle arrived next. A domestic long-haired cross, he is top cat in the house and probably in the local area too. With an air of superiority, Pickle only has to look at the other cats and they instantly give him respect.

He is intelligent and affectionate but also quite strange. Instead of grooming himself, he will jump onto your lap, lick your hand and then push his head into your hand, so you are in fact doing the grooming. He also loves to lick your nose, possibly returning the grooming favour. Unfortunately with his sandpaper tongue the experience can be rather uncomfortable.

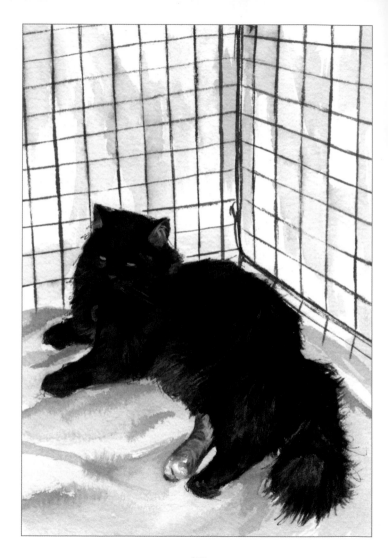

# Pickle

## Pickle is also incredibly brave.

On one occasion he hadn't been seen since breakfast: very unusual for a cat who is normally in and out all day. Diane called and called, then, late into the afternoon, he returned home barely able to walk. Diane scooped him up and rushed him to the vets. An X-ray showed he'd been shot in the back leg at very close range with an air gun. The pellet had shattered the bone inside his leg. An operation to save his leg would mean putting a rod through the leg and screwing this to the bone to allow the bone to fuse together. The leg would be shorter and he would need a fixator on the outside of his leg with steel rods. These rods would need careful cleaning twice a day for at least six weeks.

The Johnsons knew they had to try: Pickle had scaled a six-foot fence with his injuries just to get back to them. The operation took five hours to perform and the next ten weeks trying to keep Pickle in a cage were horrendous for everyone, but thankfully he made a full recovery.

However, the following year he was accidentally squashed when playing with Jasmine the Newfoundland puppy. Pickle's hock joint on the other back leg had fractured and the poor soul had another operation.

Suffering with arthritis but with his character unchanged, Pickle is still number one at home and in the neighbourhood.

# Sweets

**Sweety Plumpkin Wazza Delala Flopdown International, or Sweets, for short, has had an emotional start in life.**

Rehomed on two previous occasions, she was not enjoying much luck. The first family returned her – having had a new baby and unable to cope with both, Sweets was no longer wanted.

A beautiful female tortoiseshell, she has a perfect split chin, half sand, half chocolate. Sweets also has a strange tail which only goes out to the right – either a problem from birth or an earlier accident. She doesn't jump too well and detests being picked up.

When Sweets met Hilary Wili, life instantly got better and Hilary made a solemn vow that Sweets would never have to endure rejection again.

Sweets is an indoor cat and has little interest in exploring the outside world, although she did enjoy using the cat ladder that Hilary erected between the two balconies of her flat.

Unfortunately, an unwelcome big tom took a shine to Sweets, her ladder and her cat food. Despite changing the clap flap to open only in response to Sweets' microchip, the damage had been done and she refused to go out there again.

She is also a very fussy eater but does have a penchant for hazelnut yoghurt and a sneaky lick of a Dorito. Sweets is Hilary's best friend and although she will always be a nervous cat, she is quite contented with her new life and enjoys sitting on the window ledge, idly watching the world go by.

# Henry

## Hatching a cunning plan to ensure he stayed at Battersea's Old Windsor site, Henry the yard cat did not want to be adopted.

Brought into the Home as a stray, he was microchipped, but his original owner did not want him back. He was adopted within weeks but then returned almost immediately having bitten his new owner. Strangely, Henry had never once shown any form of aggression towards other cats, members of staff or any of the volunteers. His bad behaviour was assumed to be a one-off and Henry went back up for adoption.

Again he was rehomed, but this time he hadn't even left the cattery before sinking his teeth into the hand of his new would-be owners. As the Home had been without a yard cat for sometime, it was decided Henry

could have the job. His cunning plan had worked. Henry excelled in his new working role: friendly with visitors and staff, there were no further signs of aggression. He loved his freedom but always remembered to turn up at the cattery kitchens for breakfast, dinner, supper and tea!

Then tragedy stuck. Henry was hit by a car and killed instantly. Subsequently, staff discovered that he had regularly visited the farm across the road. Henry had been on his way over, possibly for elevenses, when the accident had happened. There was admiration as well as sadness for Henry – he was a spirited cat who had taken control of his own destiny and lived happily by his own rules.

# Percy Chatterjee

## Alison heard Percy Chatterjee before she met him.

Sitting anxiously, like a prospective parent in the waiting room at Battersea, Alison was introduced to a yowling, spitting, crazy-looking cat who was all legs and tabby stripes.

Released from his basket, he dashed madly around the small room. Then with claws spread open like bat wings, he made a frightening leap towards Alison's throat. Changing direction at the very last moment, he swung left onto her shoulder. Bemused by Alison's lack of fear, Percy Chatterjee was intrigued. At last, a worthy contender? He decided to try out her home.

Half Bengal, it was Alison who added Chatterjee, the Bengali equivalent to Smith, to Percy's name, in an attempt to make him feel a bit more at home in the wilds of Hertfordshire. His first few weeks in the Harvey household were interesting. Percy Chatterjee threw his weight around, snarling at whoever got in his way. Narrowing his great big green eyes, he'd fix you with a stare and only a clever countermove of distraction would save you from attack.

Percy Chatterjee would go walkabout for days, roaming far and wide over the fields. Petulant, independent and an adolescent bully, Percy was boss, needing no one. However, there were subtle signs that Percy Chatterjee was beginning to mellow. The good life, the freedom, the love of a good home, all were slowly chipping away at his raw edges and calming the angry young cat.

# Foxy

## And then Foxy, a Somali cross arrived at the Harveys' home.

She was adopted from Battersea's Old Windsor site, and took one look at the swaggering Percy Chatterjee and let forth a stream of cat abuse, hissing, growling and spitting.

Percy was transfixed and then, to everyone's surprise, he started shaking, turned tail and made a dash for cover. Had Percy Chatterjee met his match?

It certainly seems that way. Four months later, Foxy most definitely rules the roost. Aptly named, her fluffy red coat makes her look like a miniature fox. She was brought into the Home as a stray but when her owners were contacted, they no longer wanted her. Foxy loves cuddles and adores human company, pirouetting around, purring madly, doing anything to grab attention. In complete reverse, she detests other cats and guards her territory fiercely. However, the feline population gets off relatively lightly in comparison to her dislike for dogs. If a canine happens to walk past the house, she sprints to the window, puffing herself up as she starts her anti-dog tirade.

Percy's reaction to all this? Well, he knows he has been truly beaten by girl power and now opts for the quiet life, enjoying snoozes on Alison's bed or her work desk.

As for roaming far and wide, he still enjoys a good walkabout but if he spots anyone in the family coming home in the car, he'll hitch a lift back to the house and insist on being carried indoors.

# Pumpkin

When Vicky took on the task of hand rearing two abandoned kittens, she had no idea of the emotional rollercoaster she was about to embark on.

Casper and Pumpkin were approximately three weeks old and Vicky had been warned that they might not live because they were so young. Also, Pumpkin had an odd-shaped chest, which could dramatically reduce his chances of growing properly.

There were many sleepless nights, willing both kittens to drink enough milk to survive. At six weeks they had a heart check, were putting on weight and seemed to be doing well. However, Pumpkin was still in danger due to his mis-shaped chest and he was not put up for rehoming; it was unclear if he would survive the neutering anaesthetic and it was possible he had other abnormalities. Casper was rehomed to a loving family when he was nine weeks old, leaving Pumpkin on his own. Vicky continued fostering Pumpkin until he was old enough to be neutered, and he came on in leaps and bounds, literally, climbing up furniture and swinging off the curtains!

When Vicky received the call to say Pumpkin had made it through his operation she had never been so relieved in her whole life. After four months of tender loving care, Vicky couldn't bear to see him go and thankfully, was allowed to keep him.

There may still be other abnormalities as yet unknown, but Pumpkin seems fit, healthy and full of mischief, and Vicky wouldn't change him for the world.

# Punkie

## Malfalda Hay works in Battersea's Lost & Found department and can easily relate to pet owners' anguish, having lost her very own cat Punkie.

She had adopted Punkie and Snitch as kittens from a litter whose mother had supposedly already been neutered.

Some years later Malfalda moved house and believing both cats were happily settled in their new home she let them out to explore their surroundings. Snitch came back but Punkie didn't. Malfalda was devastated; she tried all the obvious lines of enquiry but to no avail. After months of hope Malfalda finally accepted that Punkie was gone and she closed her mind off from all the possible scenarios of Punkie's fate.

Six years later, whilst at work, Malfalda received an internal call and was astounded to hear that they had an old ginger and white cat believed to be hers. She had microchipped both her cats and on scanning, the mystery moggie's details came up as Punkie, owner Malfalda Hay.

Apparently Punkie had been living just four streets away from her old home. The owners sold the house and moved on and didn't take Punkie with them. The new occupants owned a dog and had no time for the tiresome cat that kept trying to get in. She was brought into Battersea and Malfalda was finally reunited with her 20-year-old cat who seemed none the worse for her 'walkabout' and settled back into her old home as if she had never been away.

# Jasmine

## You can wait a lifetime for a loving home and then two come along at once.

Sweet Jasmine had been a Battersea resident for over a year, so they featured her plight on their website and that's when Kate and Jeremy saw her. Unfortunately so did someone else. However, both couples were going away on holiday and neither could reserve her till they got back. It all came down to who would return first.

As a result of a painful tooth emergency, Kate and Jeremy's holiday was cut short and while Jeremy sat in the dentist's chair, Kate raced to Battersea. She got there first and Jasmine was theirs.

She settled in immediately. Stepping out of the basket, she jumped onto the kitchen worktop and sat by the kettle as if waiting for a cup of tea. When Jeremy returned home from work, she leapt onto the back of the sofa and rested her head against his. She was finally home.

Then, more good news: Kate and Jeremy were expecting their first child. Jasmine stayed close to Kate throughout her pregnancy, curling up next to her tummy and keeping her calm. When their baby son was born, Jasmine became his nurse nanny, tapping Kate's ankle whenever she heard him crying. Their relationship is delightful, his face lighting up when Jasmine pops in to check on his bedtime feed. Jasmine is loved by all and it goes to show, many good things can come from toothache!

# Poppy

Poppy – 'guardian of the photocopier' – holds the record for Battersea's oldest resident matriarch.

She came in nearly twenty years ago on Armistice Sunday, hence her name, and was assessed as too wild to be rehomed, but to the astonishment of staff, the Home's secretary, Shirley, offered her a refuge in the offices.

So Poppy joined the payroll and although she has mellowed over time many experienced kennelhands still declare their photocopying 'not really that urgent' when confronted with Poppy, stretched out on the warm copier glass, one eye open, ready to swipe.

Her office antics are legendary. She insisted on attending all the weekly meetings, scooting around the boardroom table, sending paper flying. In the early days of the computer system when a long print-out was produced at the end of each day, Poppy would appear from nowhere as soon as the printer started chugging away. As the paper spewed laboriously from the ancient machine and folded itself neatly on the floor, she would fling herself onto it, challenging anyone to move her. This resulted in the printer jamming and the whole report having to be re-run. Rather amusing in hindsight but totally infuriating at the time.

Poppy is now in retirement, enjoying her pension. Her position is still vacant and it must be said that the office environment is missing a certain frisson, an alertness that kept everyone on their toes. She is a living legend and one of Battersea's greats.

# Pluto

## Every theatre needs a cat and Battersea Arts Centre is no exception.

Hilton was renamed Pluto after a production that was playing when he arrived. Confident, with a great love of people, Pluto was the perfect choice for a bustling, theatre life and settled in very quickly. Pluto revels in the attention from staff and visitors but often seems to prefer boisterous play to mollycoddling affection. A particular favourite pastime is launching himself at the fake trees in the foyer and gripping tightly to the painted trunks.

Pluto has a great life. With sets and props from numerous productions at the BAC spread all over the building, he has limitless fun exploring all the interesting spaces created, squeezing in and out of the nooks and crannies.

He installed a rota system for his feeding and litter requirements and is pleased with how well everyone has managed it. During holidays he selects the 'chosen one' to spend quality time with him and takes full advantage of soft sofas and television before returning to work.

Pluto has acquired the habit of walking into big meetings and stealing the show at the most dramatic moment, usually by climbing onto the table – a true theatre cat!

After a long and exiting day of adventuring round the BAC, Pluto likes to relax by the fireside where he can keep a watchful eye on all the comings and goings. A playful and somewhat naughty character, he has definitely carved his own niche at the BAC.

# Posie

## If you want to know anything about cats or football, Margaret Ralph is the lady to call.

A dedicated QPR supporter, Margaret is also a full-time cat socialiser for Battersea's Old Windsor site. Taming the untameable and rehoming the unhomeable, Margaret has secured countless second chances for Battersea's feline rejects.

With a small bag of chopped chicken in her pocket, Margaret visits the cattery four or five times a week, for a couple of hours each day. Never asking anything of the cat, she simply sits and talks to them, slowly assessing their reactions and persona. Some are desperate for fuss and affection, some are incredibly shy and timid, some are fiercely aggressive to cover their fear, but, whatever they are, Margaret finds time for them all.

Posie, a Devon Rex crossed with a British Tipped, has a tiny little face and a very dense, silver coat. Wearing a permanent expression of vexation Posie is in fact very mild natured. She was four when she was given in to Battersea and had been kept in a pen all her life.

Believing Posie would benefit from a companion, Margaret adopted Pickle, a small white cat with black Turkish Van markings. Pickle had come into the Home because she didn't get on with other cats. However, she simply adored Posie and the two swiftly became inseparable. Posie had never been in a garden and it was Pickle who showed her how to climb a tree and Margaret who had to help her get down!

# Pickle

## Everyone loved Pickle and she loved everyone right back.

Winding her body affectionately around your legs, she would leave a band of white hair on your trousers, and it was then that you knew you'd been 'Pickled'.

Pickle had damage to her ears and ran a high risk of cancer. She had a mark on her ear that was pre-cancerous and whenever she went out, Margaret plastered her ears with Factor 30. Thankfully Pickle was predominantly an indoor cat. When the spot turned cancerous she had the tip of her ear removed. Then she was diagnosed with cancer of the throat and underwent chemotherapy for eight months. During that time she also suffered a stroke and Margaret truly believed that was the end, but amazingly Pickle went into remission and enjoyed another

fourteen months of life before eventually succumbing to cancer of the lungs.

Tabitha arrived next. A tortoiseshell and white kitten, she was given in to the Home with her mother and five sisters. The family were moving home and couldn't take seven cats with them. Sweet-natured, long-legged Tabitha looked nothing like her sisters, who were all small and black.

Lizzie was number four. Given in to Battersea with her brother, she was an elderly black and white cat with a bald ring around her tail and neck. No one had shown any interest in her, but that didn't worry Lizzie: she had decided to live with Margaret and began following her everywhere until Margaret brought her home.

# Pollyanna

## Lizzie enjoyed thirteen months before dying quite suddenly from pancreatitis.

Tabitha had adored old Lizzie and kept searching for her. She had seen her departure in the cat basket but not her return. Tabitha and Posie were very unsettled by the whole event and it was a long time before they went near the cat carrier again.

Pollyanna arrived a few months after Lizzie's loss. Margaret had rescued her as a play friend for Tabitha, who having lost her closest friend had become jealous, and at times, nasty to the other cats. Pollyanna was a very naughty, strong-willed little kitten. A very dark, chocolate brown semi-long-haired cat with a huge tail and green eyes, Pollyanna has perfected her evil look and uses it to great effect whenever the mood takes her.

Now nearly eight, Pollyanna has settled down but still has her likes and dislikes with the other cats, and isn't afraid to show them although she rightfully behaves herself when with the old moggies.

Serena was number six. She was suffering with a bad skin condition and had an open sore on her back from a flea allergy, all made worse from the stress of being in the cattery. The Battersea staff worked hard on Serena but she was making slow progress so Margaret offered her a home. A white cat with black markings, Serena now has a beautiful coat of fur. Despite being affectionate with Margaret, Serena can be very unpredictable and nervous, and enjoys her own space.

87

# Mia

## Number seven was Mia. She was given in by a family after reacting against the birth of a second baby.

Quickly rehomed, Mia was returned to Battersea for messing in the house. Rehomed a second time, Mia lasted three weeks before finding herself back in the cattery, again for messing.

Luckily Mia liked other cats so Margaret took her home and was surprised to find Mia was actually very clean and always used her litter tray. It was then that Margaret discovered Mia suffered from colitis: her accidents were unintentional. Mia is a lovely, playful cat, except, that is, if you try and groom her – she detests it. Margaret has had more hand injuries from Mia than all the Battersea 'ferals' put together.

Arriving on Shakespeare's birthday, Portia was number eight. A silver, short-haired, chinchilla lookalike, Margaret felt she would make an ideal companion for Posie, and she was right – Portia made a beeline for Posie and they have been the best of friends ever since.

Next to be adopted was Old Millie. A seventeen-year-old tortoiseshell, she was brought into the Home when her elderly owner passed away. The vets concluded that Millie had a heart condition and it was very unlikely she would find a new home. So Margaret adopted her and one year on, Millie is still going strong. She loves sleeping on Margaret's head and is a great mentor for the naughty kitten youngsters, speedily putting them in their place.

# Jessie

## And then there was Angel, a black and white stray cat with kidney problems.

An outdoor cat, she lived with Margaret for thirteen days before sadly passing away. It is of some comfort to know that her last days were spent in the garden, soaking up the sunshine and enjoying her freedom.

Jessie was the eleventh to arrive. Born in the wild, the mother cat was tame but the young Jessie had never been handled. Hanging off the wire, eyes wide with fear, no one could get near her. The mum was rehomed but Jessie was left behind.

Margaret had spent a great deal of time sitting and talking to Jessie, teaching her how to play, but Jessie rarely came out of her basket and showed no interest in other people. It was beginning to look like Jessie was a lost cause, but then staff noticed Jessie reacting to Margaret's voice, and straining to see her.

Margaret hesitated in adopting Jessie because she was so much younger than the others, but it was a slight hesitation and soon Jessie was happily settled into the Ralph household, bonding with the other cats and discovering the pleasures of being groomed.

So there you have it, the Ralph cat family history – eleven cats in ten years and every single one a girl. Furry, feline bliss!

# William & Mozart

## William was nicknamed Shakespeare because he is so intelligent and dignified.

He had been at Battersea twice before being adopted by Charlie and Maria.

Painfully shy, William would flee to his hiding spot under the bed if anyone came to visit. He even needed comfort and reassurance to eat. Charlie and Maria would take it in turns to sit with him as he ate: only then would he finish his food.

Worried about William's lack of confidence and that he might be lonely, they consulted Battersea and decided to adopt a playfellow. The beautiful little Mozart arrived, a gorgeous tabby with stunning tiger stripes. Contradicting all cat theories, Mozart immediately assumed the role of top cat and William didn't twitch a whisker. The day they met, William began cleaning the young Mozart and then they both curled up on the bean bag and fell asleep.

They have been best friends ever since, chasing and pouncing on each other, miaowing together, sleeping together and even visiting the vets together. If William hears Mozart cry, he'll find him and start cleaning him. William has grown remarkably in confidence, quite unrecognisable from the cat who first entered their home. If people visit, instead of taking flight, he now laps up any fuss and attention, of which there is always plenty.

William's happiness is all thanks to Mozart. Named before Maria and Charlie adopted him, it was a perfect choice as he is the most vocal, musical cat they have ever known.

# Kitten Munchkin

## Kitten Munchkin was found starved, dirty and very weak.

She was wandering the streets at an age when she should have been curled up next to her litter mates and snuggling into the warmth of a loving mother.

Jo Hasse knew immediately that this was the scraggy little bundle of fur she needed in her life and took on the role of surrogate mum. Kitten Munchkin was suffering from cat flu and failing to put on any weight. She didn't seem to know how to eat and in desperation Jo even got down on her hands and knees in front of the food bowl and tried to show her.

Kitten couldn't close her mouth and her cold wasn't clearing; her life energy was slipping away. Once more Jo returned to her local vet. Looking inside Kitten Munchkin's mouth showed

an unusual swollen palate. An exploratory investigation revealed the cause of the problem: a polyp in her throat and ear, the size of a man's thumb. Removing the polyp meant losing her left eardrum. Kitten's ear was reattached for cosmetic appearance but the poor little cat looked liked she had been hit by a bus.

However, within hours of the operation, Kitten was back home, exploring every room inch by inch, able to smell scents for the very first time. She devoured the biggest plate of freshly chopped chicken and when she'd finished, politely demanded more. After a few days Jo realised she had the cheekiest, naughtiest, happiest little cat in the world. A true survivor.